Teach Thissen Tyke

by
Austin Mitchell

Dalesman Books
in association with
Yorkshire Television
1989

The Dalesman Publishing Company Ltd.,
Clapham, Lancaster LA2 8EB

First published (by Frank Graham) 1971
This edition 1987
Reprinted 1989
© Yorkshire Television Ltd. 1971
© Additional material, Austin Mitchell 1987

Drawings by Scott Dobson

ISBN: 0 85206 921 9

Dedication

To Her Royal Yorkshire Highness the Princess Ferguson, Duchess of Yorkshire, Care of The Palace, London (By Appointment).

Uniform with this volume
"Yorkshire Jokes" by Austin Mitchell

Printed in Great Britain by
Peter Fretwell & Sons Ltd., Goulbourne Street, Keighley, West Yorkshire.

Na then Royal Thee

THA mun nivver ask a Yorkshireperson if ees a Yorkshireman. 'Appen ee is. Then ee'll tell thi' int' first words. 'Appen ees not. Then tha'll only embarrass an' 'umiliate 'im. Tha's not. Tha'll atta learn if tha's ter mek owt o' thissen. Ah'm bahn ter tell thi 'ow. So pin back thi royal lugs.

First welcome to t'land o't'Free. Nowt else is. We are. Particularly wi' advice.

Ah've not met thee. But ah've 'eard thi speyk. An tha's more Sloane 'ner Slowitt. So tha's got a lot ter live down. Tha can learn. But if tha's any ambition tha'll want ter be a Tyke. As that great Yorkshire poet John 'Artley said:

"There's a divinity that doth shape a Yorkshireman

Rough hew im ow we may."

Even if tha'll allus ave to feel a bit inferior like, tha'll want ter live i' God's Own County, now tha's Duchess of it. Tha'll want ter speyk wi't fowk. Not ter say much at first, tha's a woman, but ter listen.

Listen long. Yorkshire fowk are men of few words (an' t'women o' none). Most o' them are "bugger off". Them words we dispense so sparingly is us own, an no bugger else's. Which is why we don't chuck em around. There's too many lesser breeds wi'out t'country all waiting t'tek us words, us brass, us ideas, us fowk, us jobs, an' leave us wi' us keck bottoms 'anging out. But they've left us wi' two things. Us pride. An t' fact that Thatcher nivver cums near.

So cop this. Ah've written this little Yorkshire Primer, *Notes for Intending Immigrants*. Like thee. It's a grammar, dictionary, elocution guide, *Vade Theecum* and Phrase book. Just for thee. It'll tell thi about t'funny ways ert' fowk tha rules ovver. It'll show thi why they're t'best in't world. If they ivver condescend to say summat ter thee, as a mere woman, it'll 'elp thi ter say summat back. Even if its only bugger off. Agean.

Tha's a bit on a flibbetygibbet. Not limp under t'cap like thi brother i'law. It's just that tha dunt know ner better. Life int' meant to be all fun, fish and finerks. So get thissen a dose of reality. Arthur Scargill, an' real fowk not Southern nerks. Come ter Yorksher. Make thi 'ome ere. There's lots o' back to backs. Tha can knock a row or two together an tha'll get a back Palace Yard an'all for t'price of a Corgi Kennel in't smoke. It'll be t'mekkin of thi. Thi kids can play for Yorkshire — t' lads o' course, t'lasses go t't'mill. Tha can find out what life's all about. Tha can speyk to some marvellous people. Tha can rule ower t'loveliest parts o't'world; Barnsla, Rotherham, 'eckmendwike, Donnie, t'Dales, Sowerby Brigg. Tha can see Yorkshire NW1 i'Arrogate, Quiche Yorkshire i'Ebden Bridge. Romantic Yorkshire

3

Us Poem for t' Princess

Dedicated to Princess Ferguson, Duchess of Yorkshire
By John Hartley III
Poet in Residence, Sowerby Bridge Job Centre
Former Poet Laureate, West Riding County Council (RIP)
Grand Tykonian Order (and bar)

'Cum live wi us and be us love
If Randy wean't, then gi' im t'shove
Ter York

Weer fowk tawk straight, wi'out saying much
Life's 'ard, jobs short, and t'dole 'int much
'Baht thee

Just be thissen, a reet Royal stunner
An t'tykes 'll gawp like bloody hummer
Hob Gobbed

Tha mun still learn ter speyk, an sup an't'like
Afore tha's fit ter be us Royal Tyke
Ger on wi' it

Tha tawks cut glass: all "trizers", brass an' mouth
Tha knows no back to backs, no snickets or owt such int' south
Cum ere

Yon Dukedoms not summat to sam up an'ugger off
Else t'tykes 'll all tell thee to bugger off
Damn quick

Don't tek thi'ook. Tek t'throne i'stead
'Fore Arthur grabs it for issen. An then
Park thi bum. As t'Queen, o'Yorkshiremen
Part-time

i'Wetwang, Carnaby, Wombwell, Gildersome, Drighlington. Tha can see t'beauty and t'poverty, t'soup kitchens, t'chip 'oils and t'grocery shops turned into Beau-tykes, t'dark satanic mills turned into supermarkets and plastic factories, warehouses and pornography shooting stages. If tha's really lucky tha can meet Richard Whiteley, exchange silences wi' Geoff Boycott or catch t'fumes fra' Fred Trueman's exhaust. Ah might even tek thee for a drink missen. If tha pays. It's a wonderful world. Cum and share it. And be as miserable as us. But if tha' only visits, tha's not welcome. Tha's got a chance to mek summat o' thissen. Grab it.

> **Austin Mitchell**
> **National Union of Authors, Chip-Shop Operatives**
> **and Related Trades**

Entry into Tykonia

WARNING. *Some things do not mean what they seem to mean. For instance:*
   On alighting from the Pullman at Leeds station Clarence Fitzthrowing-Smythe (Eton and Christ's) finds difficulties in making himself understood.
Porter: Weer ta bahn luv?
Clarence: Don't be impertinent my good man. I wouldn't dream of staying in a barn. Do you know where the Queens Hotel is?

5

Porter: Appen. Tha looks like t' Queen's is reight for thee.

Clarence: (by way of polite conversation). What a crowd. What's happening?

Porter: Football's loosin.

Clarence: Oh I'm sorry to hear that. I thought Leeds would win.

Porter: Nah yer great gawpead they've not lost they've won – t'match's loosin. No point in standing ont terraces warching t'daisies grow.

Clarence: Is there a train back to London immediately?

The bright pupil will of course know that "Church's loosin" does not necessarily mean God Nil, Atheists 6. To avoid misapprehensions like this you will need to master the Tyke tongue. Listen to some of the sounds you will shortly encounter –

First test your tonsils to see if there are any structural weaknesses. Say this Test Piece:

Ah were bahn dahn us ginnel as pictures wor loosin'
It wer black as t'coil oil and mucky as t'tip,
I saw t'rag and bone man all brussen wi'boozin'
Tweltin' t'osses ower t'eads wi' t'whip.

Translation:

I was making my way down a narrow passage as the crowds were exiting from the cinema. It was extremely dark and there was mud underfoot. I saw a scrap metal merchant somewhat the worse for drink and he was belabouring his trusty steeds on their heads with his whip.

Obviously you need language classes. So read on and TEACH THISSEN TYKE.

Speykin Generally

YORKSHIREMEN are unique. They're bloody lucky to have been born in God's Own County. They speyk Yorksher. Some speyk broad Yorksher, others narrow gauge, but we've all got a bit of it.

Yorksher is a language, not a dialect. Two German parachutists were dropped on Barnsley during the war to sabotage the vital Black Pudding Factories. As they busily disguised themselves, rubbing wippet oil into their boots, two Barnsla lads passed, talking about a lass.

"Oo war she wi?"
"She war wi ersen"
"Oh washee"

The parachutists shot themselves, thinking they'd landed in China. But us is bi no means insular . . .

Take the scene at the United Nations General Assembly. Over to the interpreter: "Now the Yorkshire delegate is taking the rostrum. And, yes, he's beating it with his clog. Once, twice, three times. Now he's beginning his speech."

Maister Percy De, Wotiver tha name is, an lveuybody
Perez De Cuella, Fellow members.
Ah'm bahn atta ave a call wit t'other
I must meet urgently
grate powers, America an Russia. I Yorksher we're reet flummoxed
with American and Russia. Yorkshire is worried —
missen, ussens, thersens. Ah've allus thowt London guvanment couldn't
all of us. I was sure the government in London
organise a piss up in a brewery, they're that limp under t'cap
was incapable
but nah they've stuck their fillings inter Yorksher.
but now they've interfered with our sovereign independence
We can't reckon what they're laiking at, but they're bahn ter
for no reason we can understand.
pawse us int cods. Sitha they've got agate tekkin bits on Yorksher
They'll do us harm. They've taken bits of Yorkshire
ter gie em ter Lancashire an Durham. They've sam med Barlick
into Lancashire and Durham. They've taken Barnoldswick
ant fells to hugger em off, chip oils, pay oils, cloises an
and carried it off lock, stock and
fowk an all. They've took us jobs, us brass, us County Councils.
barrel. They have weakened us economically and abolished our County
  Councils.

7

It's fair got us capped. Ah sez ter t'barmpots i
We are puzzled. I tell Her Majesty's Government that
London we're nivver barn ter tek it liggen dahn. If it cums ter
we object. If it reaches
fratching we're not flayed. We'll a them clumping gormless set
conflict we have no fear. Her Majesty's Government
pots knackered i no time afore we giup. So Gerrof. An Gerrome.
will meet with strong resistance in its declared intention. Desist.
An ah war telled t' get thi ter gi' us us seat on t' Security Council."
My people demand their independence and recognition by the U.N.

(Wild applause from Russian delegate. All others join in singing *Ilkla Moor Baht Thatcher*).

Yorksher is a language in its own right. It has its own grammar, vocabulary and literature. With the help of this *Shorter Yorksher Primer* you'll be able to Teach Yourself Yorksher in a matter of a few days. Follow the text, do the exercises, soak your tonsils in Websters and you'll soon be understood at the Grimethorpe Sports and Social Club. With a flat'at and sewn up trouser pockets, you could even pass for a native.

History of Yorkshire Language and Literature

YORKSHIRE is the cradle of civilisation. Careful archaeological work carried out by the National Coal Board shafting some of the world's richest seams have pointed to chip oils and druidical circles (C&IU Affiliated) older than those in Sumeria, or on the Euphrates. The Yorkshire language as she is speyken is the oldest living language still continuously spoken. Or rather muttered. It has been muttered here longer than either Urdu or Hindi. Unlike them it pre-dates Indo European.

Only now is the length and brilliance of the history of Yorkshire civilisation becoming known in informed circles, in the Archaeologist's Arms. And beyond. That it is so is largely due to the expert researches and numerous publications (C.O.D.) of Albert Gaukroger, Professor of Archaeology, Advanced Brewing and Deep Fat Frying, at the *College of Tetley Technology* in Heckmondwike, PCW (Provident Customers Welcome).

Gaukroger was a man of few words. Most of those were unprintable. Yet once the beer stains have been removed from his papers and the betting slips eliminated by radio carbon dating, the narrative he took so much trouble to research, the rise of Yorkshire, can be pieced together.

The ancestor of humanity's finest flowering, the Yorkshireman, was called

Tykonian Man. He arrived in the area in the first (Pre Bird's Eye) Ice Age, coming over from the Continent of Europe on foot. The seas were already there but he was unable to afford a one way ticket on Townsend Thorreson and might not have made it in any case because the ferries weren't actually running. As a Yorkshireman he could walk over with dry feet. If the sea gets any more polluted he'll soon be able to walk back again.

The linguistic inheritance of Tykonian Man is shown in the cry the Tykonian people uttered on first glimpsing their new home. This is preserved today in such place names as Eckington, Heckmondwike or simple Heck. This Yorkshire cry of joy on glimpsng this C&IU affiliated version of paradise is not to be confused with the later Latin "Ecce Homo" meaning, "I have certain suspicions of this person." Even now people swear "By Heck" believing, erroneously, that he is the patron saint of the county.

The Tykonian People rapidly tamed the local wild life: Whippeticus Magnus, Carthortiensis, Crappingus Cowicus, Racingpidgeonius and the Backwardus Flying Duckicus of Pudsey.

There not being much to do in Yorkshire at the time they also discovered the technique known locally as Leg-Ower, or reproduction technology which later descendants perfected into that fine art which today flowers only in Yorkshire, and there only on Sunday afternoon. Which is why Sunday school was invented.

As the people became more numerous in their original landing place of Scarborough (where our tribal homing instinct still takes us back), their leaders urged them to go forth and multiply. Or as they put it in the language of the time to "F(the word is indecipherable in the manuscript) Off." They did and settled in different parts of their wonderful new home. Gradually they divided up into tribes, mostly huddled back to back for warmth though to huddle in any other way might have increased population pressures.

The Millworkus tribe lived in the West Riding and loom large in the history of the county. The Mineworkus tribe lived in the south of the county and worked in the black economy appearing above ground only after dark because of their ugliness. The Dockworkus tribe were the most striking of all, though somewhat less mobile than the rest and all too readily identified in prehistoric rape cases because the women had to do all the work. The Steelworkus tribe lived round Sheffield and Rotherham but also found overflow accommodation in Scunthorpe and Middlesbrough. The Fishworkus tribe lived all down the East Coast and eventually in one of the first daring circumnavigations of the known world they discovered Fleetwood but they wisely thought it better to close down in the next Ice Age leaving it uninhabitable. Which it has remained to this day. Finally came the Landladies, stood by all along the coast to repel boarders.

Each tribe had its own chief or "Gaffer", and "Bard" — a word later corrected to "Board" before being privatised to "nowt". The exceptions were the Millworkus tribe. At first they lived at the top (attus topus) of the hills where there was room. They then moved down to the valleys for more efficient sewage disposal and to use the canteens of the newly developed "Mills".

This division into tribes was kept up long after they discerned Romans in the gloaming. Indeed it still survives, despite the efforts of Mrs. Thatcher to reduce us all to one tribe, the P45 People. The Romans and Gastronomans were lured in by the worldwide reputation of such native delicacies as Pie and Peas, Black Puddens and that apogee of the art Yorkshire Puddens. These made Yorkshire the centre of the culinary world. So the Romans invaded to get control of the Pudden Supply points and inflicted the only defeat ever sustained by the Tykonian people in their long and glorious history. They broke up the Kingdom of Elmet by moonlight, and spread their power right up to the Tweed (Roman name: *Lentheric*) on the east and to Cockermouth (Roman name: *Fellatio*) on the west.

Caesar divided Yorkshire into three parts. Or Ridings. An arrangement which lasted until Pete Walker. Yet Yorkshire was no longer independent. It didn't need to be because it was now the centre of the known world. York was the capital of the Yorksher Empire, sometimes erroneously referred to as the Roman Empire because the Emperors kept moving all over the place. Emperor Severus set up his palace on a site there which is now occupied by the Railway Institute, though the Yorkshire Empire wasn't built in a day because it was done by direct labour. However, the Emperor Constantime (the inventor of Greenwich Mean Time as well as the one-way chariot system in York, in which some chariots are reputed to be still stuck) was born in York. He ruled his empire from there with the help of a worldwide pigeon service organised from Barnsley where the birds were processed into pies on their return.

Unfortunately not enough Yorkshiremen were promoted to positions of power in the empire. They refused to leave the best part of it and weren't paid a rehousing allowance. So the empire declined. Yorkshire reverted to being a self-governing province, the first self-governing republic where the writ of King Arthur did not run. No one could read it. Camelot was ignored because it wouldn't move to Barnsley. The republic was then invaded by the Angles who were acute enough to know a good county when they saw it. Led by Hypotenuse, who was something of a square (particularly in comparison with the other two sides), and his son Obtuse from whom we inherit our bluntness, they came over from Germany to get away from the Common Market. It was not only dead common but was also passing directives to keep down the noise in rape and pillaging parties. So they added a new stock to our genes, particularly to those Jeans who knew all the Angles.

They brought with them the newly developed "sheep" which relieved a lot of unemployment among the Millworkus tribe in the West Riding and gave names to a whole list of places deliberately kept blank on the map such as Shipley, Shepley, Sheepscar and D'Ewesbury. The chief areas settled by the Angles have been carefully identified by the Cleckhecktonsedge Historical (C&IU affiliated) with these signs placed by roads wherever their

researchers have been able to check the Angles.

The only subsequent migration before the Indians and Pakistanis was the Normans, a bunch of Charlies lured north to gain control of the Ossett fish docks and Pudsey Treacle mines. They found us revolting. Having easily defeated the effete southern English they met here with a resistance so vigorous that they had to invade the north, lay waste the country and destroy the towns, a technique later repeated by Mrs. Thatcher who called it "Industrial Strategy". The Normans contributed nothing to the language except "necessire" — the dirty word for shit-house. They did, however, introduce the technique known as Frog Marching which is the way we greet southerners, and the new sport of *Jus Primae Noctae*. Ingenious Yorkshiremen quickly extended this sport to the second, third, fourth and every subsequent *noctae,* having reserved for their women folk a very special place. It is known as the scullery.

The rest of the Norman legacy was malign. They gave us our long standing dislike of southerners usually detectable because, like the Normans, they smell of garlic rather than wool grease. They introduced the condom which made us even happier than we were already but kept the population down. They pioneered the class system, dividing free Yorkshiremen who had hitherto been equal and had always believed that Jack was not only as good as his master but probably better, into High Yorkshiremen (called Norman, Cecil or Cedric) living in Harrogate and the North Riding, Middle Yorkshiremen who owned the mills, pubs and fish shops and Low Yorkshiremen who worked, drank and ate in them (unfortunately rather indiscriminately). They lived in back to backs and terrace houses to cut down their heating bills and were called Fred.

The rest of Yorkshire's history is uneventful. The world intrigued, plotted, fought wars. Empires rose and fell. Yorkshire got quietly on with its job of mekkin a bob or two. We didn't need to prove our courage, virility or fashionableness. We were happy making what the rest of the world needed, living comfortably in the most beautiful part of an increasingly nasty world. Occasionally we sent the odd Yorkshireman south, Asquith, Snowden, Harold Wilson, Denis Healey, to show them how to run things. Sometimes we sent others with even better intentions such as Guy Fawkes to put them right. We didn't belong to any organised party, we were Labour. Ever since that famous Yorkshireman Robin Hood introduced Socialism well before Karl Marx. He founded the first party branches near Wakefield and organised a Job Training Scheme in robbing the rich to feed the poor which flourished. Until Mrs. Thatcher put it in reverse.

Life in Yorkshire was an idyll. And so were most of us. Even if we didn't know what the word meant. Left on our own we were happy, though of course in Yorkshire that's a relative term. The idyll was ended by interference from outside. They closed down us mines and us mills. They took away us gas. They abolished us Ridings, introduced some new insanity no one could understand and then abolished that. They gave us fish to t' Common Market. They scrapped the Jowett car to stop us rivalling Detroit and closed the Holmfirth film industry when it was threatening Hollywood. They gave us men their P45s and us women uppety ideas about how a woman's place isn't on her back. Yorkshire has been bashed, buggered and bewildered. The time has come to fight back. A spectre is haunting London. It's the spectre of Yorkshire, uniting under the battle cry of 'Ome Rule. Yorkshiremen of the world unite. You have nothing to lose but your unemployment benefit, intermediate grants, *East Enders* on telly and endless lectures from London.

A Passionate Appeal

TYKONIA is surrounded by enemies all dedicated to suppressing the Tyke Tongue. To the North, the Jordyhinnians speak a form of pidgeon Scots. To the West the Lancymacassars have already begun infiltrating long vowel sounds into Todmorden, and moving slowly down the Calder Valley to encircle the vital Clog Sole Factories. To the South Subdoncastrium or Lincsanderbynotted begins at Dronfield where the wife swappers go in the winter.

Even here subversives from the E.T.U. (Elocution Teachers' Union, or the Sisterhood) have been smuggled over our borders disguised as human beings, and the BBC infiltrates the ether. In a few places like Harrogate, Yorksher as she is speyken isn't. And last week the *Barnsley Chronicle* reported that a haspirate had even been breathed there, a town where normally folk eat coal and breathe only fire. This Subdoncastrium conspiracy holds Yorkshire lads back from positions of power they'd otherwise occupy. Herbert Clogworthy would now be Archbishop of Canterbury insted of Con. Sec. at the Glasshaughton Working Men's Club, Joe Gormley would be Headmaster of Eton instead of Caretaker at St. Helen's Primary School, Monk Bretton, were there not such a strong prejudice against Yorkshire.

The time has cum to fight back. Yorksher language and literature must be made a compulsory subject in secondary schools and universities as well as chip shops and pubs. Yorksher must be the official language for all communications from local and national government within the county. Speyken tests should be imposed on all elective officials and officers. The Harry Ramsden Foundation should finance Adult Education classes in Reeding and Riting in Harrogate Working Men's Clubs. The Yorksher language must be preserved.

Here's a basic quick grammar and yammer to help you tell Yorks talk from Southern mutter. Teach thissen tyke in seven days. An join t'lads.

Primary Class

THE best start to speyking Yorksher is to begin (gerrin) wit'kids int scoils. Take Barnsley where primary scoil children begin Yorksher with the very latest teaching methods. The Subdoncastrians learn English by looking and saying with Janet and John and French by following the adventures of the famille Deranged or Desgranges or whatever. The Barnsley Association of Yorksher Taychers (Meetings Monday 8.30 at the New Lodge Hotel) has opted for *Sitha and Saytha with the Blenkinsop Family*. Take a typical page of this:

Sitha our Enoch.
Sitha our Ethel.
Sitha us Councilouse.
Sitha us Wippet. It's peed ont floor agin.
Wots up wiem saytha.
They look like a week on neets.
Our Enoch's just thumped our Ethel int breadbasket. Int ee a norty lad.
Nivver mind. Us Dad'll thump is lug. Thump is lug Dad. Thump is lug.
Sitha us Mam.
Sitha us Dad.
Us Mum's bawling agen.
Wots us mum bawling for nah saytha?
She's belling er ead off cos she war as throng as Throp's wife wen she
    anged ersen wit' dishclout when us Dad cum ome kalied agen.
Us Dad's reet sloshed.

13

Us Dad's been downt'boozer all day an spent all us brass. An it int dole day till Thursday.

Mam'll belt is ead in.

Belt is ead in Mam.

Belt is ead in.

Int it grand i Barnsley. Ee it is. Int it.

A Nexercise

Now answer these questions sitha:

Wot has Enoch done to Ethel?

Wot as Dad dun wit brass?

Wot day duz Dad sign on?

Az mam wun at Bingo?

Ow much is a cake an chips?

If you can't answer these questions you are limp under t'cap and educationally underprivileged. Watch out or you'll end up at Giggleswick or Woodhouse Grove Instant Public Schools.

On t'other 'and, them as lerns ter speyk reet can get down t' mines, werk as tatters, or go int't'black pudden factories, an mek a bob or two an sup therrsens stupid an ave a reet grand time. So stop readen't'book ere if yer've answered reet an fork out another five bob for us book on *Advanced Tyke Talking*. Sing t'Bansla Anthem an ave another pint.

Now study various examples of Tyke expression prior to further tongue-twisting. This will allow you to savour the beauties of the Yorksher thought-process:

Drunk as a Fiddler's Bitch: If quadruple Green Stamps were given for the purchase of four or more gallons of beer he would have done well to take a suitcase to the hostelry with him.

Eez peed ont chips: He has frustrated our plans. See Margaret Thatcher's comment on President Reagan's decision to bomb Libya and Bradford (where no one noticed but damaged estimated at 17p was sustained).

Strong as Chip Oil Vinegar: Me thinks he has not taken the Charles Atlas course.

As Mucky as a Sink Oil Tooad: He will never grow rich on the Divi from the purchase of a Co-op carbolic.

If ee fell oft Co-op eed fall int Divi Ole: He is a rather fortunate person. Usually applies to building workers on the lump, anyone outside the textile industry and to self employed Black Pudding Blenders.

Snap: Miner's lunch, food. When the roof is very low miners say "t'seems that low tha mun tek pancakes for thi snap."

14

Ee wudn't part wit reek ov is own muck: He is not the most generous of men. Applied usually to Scotsmen, the phrase also has some relevance in Batley.

Oil: This can be poured on almost any troubled noun as in coil oil, chip oil, lug oil, cake oil, bobby oil, pit oil, or even used with its own adjectives as in mucky oil. More complex uses: Ass oil – grate under fire place, Pay oil – Pea and Pie Shop, Slap oil – puddle, Delf oil – quarry, Bug oil – cinema like t'Pavilion i' Shipley where t'Commissionaire used ter say "Don't spit int ashtrays I want t'tab ends." But it's so long since t'Pavilion closed that yer can see t'films it used ter show on TV now. In the rest of the country the word oil has been taken over by Esso. Correct Yorkshire usage is best explained by drilling expert Arthur Blenkinsop who rose from being Under Deputy at Wombwell Main to the Most Boring Official of the N.C.B. Yorkshire Region. On a lecture tour of America Blenkinsop was asked by one smart-Alec "if holes were oils what was the stuff that came out of them?" "Grease yer daft beggar" was Blenkinsop's witty reply.

Sodjer: Means soldier if applied to someone in uniform. If applied to someone out of uniform it can be assumed not to be a compliment.

You are now ready to proceed further into the mysteries of the Tyke tongue so get yer glottalstops ready an GETSTUCKINLAD.

US DAD

15

Getting Thissen Fit

LANGUAGE reflects character. This is a hard county. It breeds hard folk who speak a language of hard sounds. Yorksher is more wearing on the mouth than any other Lingua Franca, ask Frank himself. This is why we talk less. When Tykonian Man arrived in the Bird Eyes Age the first sound he uttered was g-g-g-g. The hard G has remained with us ever since. Consonants are the landmarks of language. They have to be given prominence and tret hard. Like shunting engines they are for conveying one batch of minor sounds to or from another.

Southerners pronounce G with the front of the mouth. We use the back so it has to be specially reinforced. Those not born with the double gauge corrugated roof can take strengthening treatment by taking a West Riding County Council road sweeper's brush that's seen good service down Carr Lane, dipping it in best creosote, igniting and then brushing the back of the mouth and the tonsils vigorously. As you take the brush out you will already be pronouncing the Yorkshire G-g-g. The reinforcement will also allow the mouth to tolerate the Cleckheaton K-k-k. Practice both sounds carefully at first. These are sounds for men. They'll also reveal any imperfections in the rib cage.

The Tyke T't't is even more vital, being used instead of the English word "the". To acquire this in quick time: prepare a strong Madras curry sauce, stir in half an ounce of black peppers, eighteen chillies, a quarter pound of cayenne pepper and six pounds of Colman's mustard.

Heat on North Sea Gas to ensure that the thing goes with a bang and put your tongue gently into the boiling liquid. (The liquid can also be used for cauterising boots). The pain can now be eased by blowing cold air over the tongue tip while at the same time tapping it rapidly against the cool roof of the mouth. When the screams die down you will find you are making the Tyke T't't. You may also be drowning this book in spray. Carry on until you can make the sound without passing water as in "take the horse to the wooden building" which becomes TEKTOSSTUTUT.

Tykonomy

SPEYK teachers in pubs all over the county will tell you that the other key to proper speyking is ECONOMY. This is also part of our character. A bloke in Barnsley tried to compete with the supermarkets by offering an immediate money back guarantee at his grocery. One morning he was amazed when a little kid came to get his mum's money back on two toilet rolls. The explanation was quite simple: "Company didn't come."

We're as provident with language as with brass. One is chucked around like a man with no arms the other in the fashion made popular by Herbert Long who had no tongue.

These are the basic rules of Tykonomy in speyking.

1. The ideal is total silence: Ear all see all say nowt.

Some of us attain this ideal and never have to buy another round for the rest of our lives. This is known as ODDINTHINOISE or SHUTINTHICAKEOIL. All Yorkshire children take compulsory lessons in these subjects.

2. Where speech is essential a multi-purpose word which can mean whatever the hearer likes it to mean can often be used.

Southerner: "Does this road lead to Pickeringdale Pike?"
Articulate Dalesman: "'Appen."
Southerner: "Thank you my good man."

'Appen it doesn't, but then it's fun finding out. Other useful variations of the Mixendon Multinoise are "By Gum" which can be inserted into conversations at hourly intervals to show you are awake and interested, or "Eck" a contraction of the latin Ecce Homo, the pet name of Ben Dover the Civil Servant in charge of Regional Aids policies.

3. Never use a whole word where it can be contracted. "Something" takes 1.85 seconds to say "summat" 0.94 seconds. Anything and nothing can be contracted to owt and nowt, a process which gives commercial travellers from the Rosencratz Clothing and General Supply Co. in Leeds, the fastest

turnround in the country. Their conversations with shopkeepers run as follows:

"Owt?"

"Nowt"

"Tarra"

4. Where words are known to both parties in a conversation they can be dropped altogether except for some symbolic noise. Take the following early morning conversation in millions of Yorksher homes as the wife strives to get hubby down for breakfast. The old shout of "Clogs is going past" having received the traditional reply of "Put mine out and see if they'll go", the conversation carries on as follows:

Mam	"Y'up?"
Dad	"ibed"
Mam	"Grup"
Dad	"Shrup"
Mam	"Grup"
Dad	"Mup"

Us Mam and Dad can then return to the higher reaches of humour with Mam saying "It int fit ter put a dog out. Don't forget this snap." If you live in Rotherham ignore this. You'll be woken up automatically by the sound of the sparrows, coughing. Other candidates for emasculation are "will" or "have to." "Next bus'll be late tha'll atta run". By the same token "the" should be used only when talking to royalty or the manager of the Devonshire Arms at Grassington. It's not generally known that economising on "the" during the twenty third and twenty fourth Yorkshire Wars (also known as First and Second World Wars) we saved so much newsprint in Yorkshire that it was vital in winning the war. For its efforts the county was awarded the George Cross by King Edward VIII and we are officially entitled to be the Kings Cross County. T' can of course be confusing to Southerners, like the visitor to old Bradford telling the newspaper lad he couldn't remember which paper he'd preferred on his last visit but it had begun with a t. The lad replied scornfully "That dun't 'elp. There's t'Telegraph, t'Argus and t'Observer."

5. Another method of economising is to make as many things as possible singular. This allows you to replace "re" by the "Sedburgh zis" as in "Picture zis loosing". The soldiers are marching becomes "sodger zis marching". The only exception to this rule of singularity is when talking about yourself. Yorkshiremen are entitled to use the royal we, though all except Jimmy Savile have now agreed to let Mrs. Thatcher have it. We still refer to ussens as us as in "Usmam" and "Usdad" or in the passionate plea "gie us one."

6. Certain letters can be left out. The haspirate is both ateful and an eadache. It should be used only when chatting to the Hearl of Arewood over his backyard wall. The former editor of the *Pudsey Examiner* could only

18

have been a Tyke. As the season for the ducks to migrate backwards to Stanningley approached he would leap round the office hitting the staff on the head and bawling "I'm t'eaditter."

A Nexercise

You can now learn rules four, five and six by repeating four hundred times the battle cry of the 'Avercake Lads. "T'officerzis itting t'osses ower't'ead wit'whips. T'officerzis itting t'osses ower t'ead wit'whips."

7. All vowel sounds must be short and sharp. Don't ooo and aaarse around like a Young Conservative at a haunt bawl. Southerners swill vowel sounds round the gob as if savouring a fine wine "aaaay saaay ooold maaan". We spit them out which is why no one up here can sing "Kaahmen to the Garden Maud" properly. Remember:

aaaah	–	a as in knackered
uuuuh	–	u as in cum
eye	–	i as in din
ooooh	–	o as in 'og

These short, sharp noises are best produced after eating half a dozen Barnsley Black Puddings each immersed in half a pound of best mushy peas. This mixture will produce a generous supply of short sharp rushes of air, the basic raw material for good vowel sounds. Since you will be speaking from the soul it is advisable to wear Y Front underwear when practising your Yorkshire vowel sounds.

A Nexercise

Repeat the following 80 times in Yorksher, "*If there were another war this war will be worse than the last war*" It translates as"*If there war another war this war'll be war n't'last war.*"

8. The final principle of economy is to merge words together. On the bricklayer principle, examine your words. Do they look compatible. Bang them together in your mouth. Do they merge easily? Will knocking a bit off help? Where "give me" is ugly and unattractive "gimme" has a nice flow to it. So does the advanced student's "gius". Hard edges can be softened. The main techniques are:

(*a*) "have not" can be softened into 'mp' as in "Iampgorrit" (I have not got the object to which you are referring).

(*b*) F can either be left off or softened to v, a technique first perfected by the early Methodists who, tired of hostile crowd reactions in the pit villages finally agreed to the crowd's plea by leaving the f off. A request for matches, pipe tobacco, or, in Batley, money can be simplified to ASANYONYERANYONYER (has any of you gentlemen a small amount of the object in question on your person).

19

(*c*) T has done well enough out of us at the beginning of words so it can be softened at the end. Elementary students should turn it into an r. "Would you kindly remove yourself" becomes "gerroff", the courting cry of the Yorkshire mill lass. The officiating archpriest, the Con. Sec. completes this creed with the traditional response "shurrup". More advanced students can obtain the same effect by using the Glasshaughton glottal stop to complete the "t word" with silent "Glug". This technique can be mastered later.

Translation

Translate the following into English giving yourself three marks for a fully correct answer, two if one word is wrong, one for a partially right answer and none for a baffled gurgle. (Don't cheat – cover up the answers).

Standard Yorksher	*Standard Engish*
1. PUTWOODINTOIL	Kindly close the door.
2. INTITORFUL	Isn't it rather awful.
3. THADBERRERLERRERGERITERSEN	It is perhaps advisable to allow her to make her own choice.
4. YERNIVVERMISSASLICEOFFERCUTCAKE	I'm sure your husband wouldn't mind.
5. ASTERGOROWTTERGIUS	Have you anything to give us?
6. SUMMATSUPEER	Something would appear to be wrong here.

7. GERRITETTEN	Please hurry up and eat your food.
8. WASAMARRER WIIM	What, I wonder could possibly be the matter with that gentleman?
9. IAMPGORRITWIME	I have not in fact got the object to which you are referring.
10. ISEEGOINGOME	Is he about to set off for home?
11. ASTERGORRITWITHEE	Have you got the object to which I am referring with you?
12. AYAMPTEERDNOWT	I have not actually heard anything.
13. EESEZITINTISBURRABERRITIZ	He says that the object is not in fact his but I think that it is.
14. EELAFTERGIEOWWER	He will have to desist.
15. OURLASSEZGORRABUNINTOVEN	My sister appears to have conceived.
16. ATELLTIMBURREEWUDDENTLISSEN	I did in fact tell him but he was reluctant to listen.

Astergorritreit? Thenthamungerritlernt. Ahclowtthiifthaduntgerronwiit. With 48 marks thasdunreetwell. Getthipuddinetten. 35–47 tha'll do but tha'll atta spend a few neets on refresher course in any C.I.U. affiliated College of Father Education. Between 20 and 34 marks you're either trying to live down a Grammar School education or low origins somewhere just south of Doncaster.

Between 10 and 19. Go to Castleford, move directly to Castleford. Stay there. Do not collect benefit.

Below 10. You're hopeless, either a Public School man or a member of Her Majesty's Government. In the words of that witty reply, much favoured by graduates of the Grimethorpe College of Wit and Repartee, get knotted.

More Vocabulary

Bob: Until the intervention of the Decimal Currency Board this had two meanings. "If tha Bob dunt gie our Bob t'bob 'at tha Bob owes our Bob our Bob'll gie tha Bob a bob ont'nose."

Jock: Food, lunch, sandwiches. Up in Slowitt (or Slaithwaite if yer believe t'atlas) they're that daft they run t'watter an t'gas up t'same pipe. A farmlad more slow-witted than most dropped his jacket into the midden. Farmer arrived to find him poking round in the manure with a big stick trying to find it. "Nay" sez the farmer "it's no use getting thi jacket out of there, it'll reek to high heaven." "Aye" said the lad "but mi jock's int'pocket."

21

Ither: Either. Ask anyone in the Wallace Arnold Sports and Social Club at Royston whether it's Ither or Either. They'll tell you "Awther'll do."

Baht: Not only applied to 'ats on Ilkla Moor. In the 23rd Yorkshire (or First World) War a Yorkshire lad enrolled in a Somerset regiment. Asked why he was on parade without a rifle he replied "ee nivver gie us ony on em." Asked for explanation he could only say "I ant got none." This reduced the whole regiment to baffled incomprehension. At great expense an interpreter was fetched down from civilisation (actually Dodworth). After conversation with the rifleless tyke he reported to the C.O. "Well what does he mean then?" bawled the Commander. "Ee sez ees baht" said the interpreter. *When t'lads say they're "supping baht" it's your round.*

Agate: To start, get on with. When our American allies were helping in the 24th Yorkshire (or the Second World) War, by keeping our girls happy while Yorkshire lads fought the Hun, one took a Shipley lass up the Glen. "Gee honey, how about a kiss and a cuddle" he breathed passionately. "Well get agate then" she replied. When he came back with one, she'd gone off to t'Rosse for a Babycham.

Sitha: No relation to Anton Karas or the Harry Lime theme, this is a multi purpose word fulfilling much the same role as the "Now Hear This" announcement in the American Navy. Frowned on by middle class parents in Brighouse where they're that daft they put t'pig ont wall ter watch t'band go by. The Jarrat family were going up in the world. Little Richard said to his dad as they walked down Bonegate "Sitha yon bloody dog ont job." Dad replied "How many bloody times have I to tell you not to say sitha."

Allus: As in the refrain of the famous song "I'll be luving you, allus."

Neet: As in "Ah've just supped a bottle o'Whisky". "Good heavens was it neet". "Wor it eck. It wor broad dayleet."

Lame under t'cap: He is not the most intelligent of mortals. Can also be applied by people in Cleckheaton to the inhabitants of Spenborough and by those in Spenborough to denizens of Cleckheaton.

Laike; In Barnsley they'll tell you of the fish and chip shop on the New Lodge Estate where the locals all hang round on Monday, skint because the investment of their redundancy pay with William Hill has inexplicably failed to prosper. A large Rolls Royce pulls up and an upper class voice asks, "Is this the way to the Lake District". All reply with one voice, "You're there. Everybody laikes on Monday". The Castleford variation is the kid's essay on "The Great Lakes" which covers Cricket, Soccer and Rugby League. To laike is to play, from the old German lacken: drawing dole money. Ask any miner at Hoyland why he only works three days a week and he'll tell you "Cos Ah can't manage if ah laikes fer more ner two".

Nessy: Derived from the Scandinavian Nesscheisserhausen or meeting place, a place where motions are passed. Corrupted into lavatory. In the

Dales where the old fashioned thunder box is still found the Appletreewick Truant Catcher and Rodent operative called on Mrs. Robinson to reprimand her because young George hadn't been to school for six weeks. When he concluded with the warning that if this went on he would have "to take the necessary steps" she was unconcerned. "Then us'll atta do us business int'field."

Time to Visit the Natives in their Natural Habitat

MEANWHILE what about our old pal Clarence Fitzthrowing-Smythe on his safari into deepest Tykonia? As it 'appens 'ees 'overing outside one of our unique hostelries cum clubs cum social centres. At the door he is warmly welcomed by an ancient of the tribe who hockles on Clarence's booits before speyking.

Doorman: Are yer t'turn?
Clarence: I beg your pardon?
Doorman: Are yer t'artist?
Clarence: Oh are you having some kind of exhibition?
Doorman: Wot club yer from?
Clarence: Oh Clahbs. Well . . . the Athenaeum and Whites.
Doorman: Nivver eard on em. Are they filleted?
Clarence: I beg . . .
Doorman: Well oo's t'Con.-Sec.?
Clarence: Well . . . Norfolk . . .
Doorman: Eddie Norfolk! Yon old beggar fr Lower Wortley. Any pal on Eddie's is a pal o mine. Gerrin wi yer.

Inside, Clarence's lug oils will be assaulted by an electronic organ belting out *Exodus*. He'll need wellies to wade through the spilt ale, but he can't fail to be impressed by the Chargey Daffairs, the Con.-Sec. sitting in state in his box and occasionally bawling "GIUSBESTOVORDER. PLEEZ." This translates roughly as "please be quiet". He might even address himself to Clarence, as he edges nervously across the room: "Wots tha mean tha great gobslotch moochin round while Arry's obliging ont'organ. Park thiseen an give t'poor sod a chance. Ee's doin is best. Thee sidahn an belt up."

This does not mean "prepare for take off" unless Clarence has stumbled into the Sunday lunchtime strip and nature study.

Con.-Secs. can even change the names of persons and groups. One neet at the Askerne Antediluvian and Clog Puddlers' Institute a rock and roll group arrived, all long hair and million megawatt amplifiers. "What's thi name" said the Con.-Sec. "Anderson's Apocalypse" they replied. "Tha's t'Four D's toneet" he said chalking "FOWER DEES" on his blackboard.

Having found a seat, Clarence is approached by an enormous giant of a man who addresses him "Wotyergonneravluv?" Ignore the endearments.

T'Club Doorman

This is not a sexual advance and should be answered with "GiusagilloTets" or if Clarence wants to make friends, "Letsavajarallround." Clarence shouldn't be shocked if one of his new mates says to the waiter "gie us a touch luv." He wants a dash of lemonade. The drink will have brought new friends for Clarence. At first he should merely listen to what they have to say while throwing in an occasional "ByEck", "BloodyUmmer" or even "Wellallgotertopovourstairs."

As his confidence grows Clarence can even use a pause in the flow to try a phrase such as "Owerthebuggersgerrinonthen". In Bradford where excitement still lingers over City's recent (1911) F.A. Cup victory this will produce a discussion on football. In Castleford it will be taken as a reference to Cass. In the summer it will lead to an analysis of God's perversity in not giving Yorkshire "BESTOVORDER" in the weather, though possibly with an admission that he can't favour his own side too much. It may even be understood as a reference to how the Brass Band Championships have been rigged against the locals. Whatever the subject Clarence has begun a conversation.

When it ends he can immediately trigger off another and draw attention to the fact that it's someone else's round by quietly smacking his lips and murmuring "Notabadjarovaleere. Damnsiteberretnertpissahadtotherneet." Recollections and discussion will pour forth. With a bit of luck he might even get a long argument on the exact difference between London beer and lemonade. By now Clarence will be thoroughly accepted. Before he even needs to speyk again the room will suddenly fill with the Con.-Sec.'s voice interrupting Marion Golightly's rendering of "Velia oh Velia my witch of the wood" with the shout of "Cumonlads. Givtpoorcow a chance – Oh'ang on. Ah see t'pies ave cum. Yes it's mate an taty a bob, steak an kidney one an a tanner. Yes lads t'pies av cum." No more need be said. The rest of the evening is ATENSWILLTIME until the steward wishes them all "God Speed and sleep tight" with a friendly "Cumonlads. Seeyerdrinksoffnah." Clarence as dun reet well which should be some consolation for what's going to happen to his ring of confidence when he gets home.

Now some more lessons so GERAGATEANGERRONWIIT.

Nobbut a Bit More

IN general vowel sounds are short and sharp. But not when the vowels follow each other or the sound can't be shortened. Here you must employ the Drighlington dypthon. "After Dad's death I was going home down the road past the school when I saw a ghost round a post" would be translated "Atta Dad's deeath I war bahn hooam down t'rooad past t'scooil when I saw a ghoooast goin raaand a pooast." Right? Well do it again (This in fact refers to the Stanningley ghoooast which war nobbut a poooost). Where two vowels come together don't blur them, pronounce both separately as in *me-at, se-at, fo-am.* The long i sound becomes ee as in seet (sight) a pronunciation which has caused a lot of doctors to make patients take their trousers down when all they needed was optical treatment. But if it's an *ight* it becomes *eyt* as in *feyt* which isn't a garden party or something worse than death, but a bloody set too. Also O on its own when it can't be shortened to a cry of pain becomes *owa* as in the Shipley Conservative Club also known as the Towaries.

You is a sound very rarely heard in Yorkshire. Being more friendly we prefer thou, tha or in emergencies t' as in "Weer ta bahn lass" or "Where are you going to, my pretty maid." In moments of extreme anger Ossett Fish-puddlers have been known to resent thou and reply "Don't thee thou me thee thou thissen and see how tha likes thee thouing" but this is rare. Normally it's "you" that is regarded with suspicion because it looks like part of an income tax demand or some official communication. The only real problem is that with sloppy pronounciation tha can be mistaken for other words. The Yorkshire Symphony Orchestra (R.I.P.) were playing at the Heckmondwike Promenade concerts during the strike by the Cleckheaton Federation of Sewage and Related Trade Operatives. "Weer's t'arpist" demands the Conductor scanning the ranks only to have the fifth violinist bawl back "Behind t'piano, weers tha?"

Careful speyk training can eliminate this problem. In Sheffield up t'Wicker wee t'watter runs ower t'weir, they prefer dou to thou so greet people here with "Now den dee wot da doing wi di sen".

Finally there are various conjugations which can only be learnt by heart.

25

1. To bi (verb), as in Shakespeare's "to bi or not to bi". It conjugates Am, Thart, Eez, Sheez, Usiz, Yar, Themis. The negative is usually obtained by putting not at the end "I arent, tharnt, eeint, sheeint etc." Elocution teachers have worked hard to stamp out this usage. At South View Juniors, Yeadon, the teacher was taking names for the school trip, when Jack Riley loudly announced "I aren't going." He was hauled out as an example "Jack you know it should be 'I am not going, you are not going, he is not going, she is not going, we are not going, they are not going'" Jack was unimpressed. "Int no one goin then is there" he announced. Jack should have been doing the teaching "Ah sharn't an ah weyn't say owt but I aren't" is reet Yorksher.

2. The future of to bi is willa, witta, willee, willer, willus, willyer, willem.

3. To gi (verb), conjugates gimme, githee, giim, gier, gius, giem, giiower, giup, usually followed by gerroff.

4. Some verbs cause problems only in the past tense. Put becomes putten, though the class sneak in our primary school made a fool of himself when he told teacher "Miss, Austin's putten 'putten' when ee shud ave putten 'put'."

5. Missen. Visitors often assume that Mr. Missen is either Yorkshire's gaffer or its most popular personality, having misheard our toast as we raise us Dandelion and Burdock "here's to me and my wife's husband not forgetting missen." In fact he's almost as popular as Mr. Thissen for whom a lot of us will do owt for nowt. Missen was immortalised in the 24th Yorkshire war when Brian Dean, a pilot from Pudsey, who used to fly his bomber backwards was listing his crew as safe after returning from bombing the Obergurgle Saurkraut Factory. "There's Smith the Bombadier, Blenkinsop the navigator, Fotheringay-Smythe the lavatory cleaner and there's Missen," he reported, thus giving rise to the famous phrase "One of our pilots is Missen". It conjugates Missen, thissen, hissen, erssen, ussens, yersenns, thessens. Repeat this forty times until you get the sens of it. By the way if you include brussen you'll get stuffed.

Talking Tyke by Numbers

YOU are now ready to speyken thee Yorksher (or Lethigobflap). For this you need to know what to say. Stick to what's safe. Emergency wards all over the county are choked with would be linguists having bottles removed after trying concepts too advanced for their ability. So here's a guide to speyking by numbers which will allow you to make one thousand do-it-yersen Yorksher sentences. All have been tried and tested in the Batley Variety Club, Walton British Legion, and the Coal Board offices at Allerton-Byt-Water. Just pick any number with three figures, say 147 for the number of honest folk in London. Take the first phrase in column one, the fourth in two and the seventh phrase in column three and combine them to make:

"Hellsbells an buckets o'blood but t'aint true as work killed no one cos even osses turn ther arses to it dont yer reckon." This will (*a*) Identify you as a true tyke-talker and (*b*) get a conversation going with whatever natives you care to address it to and (*c*) commit you to nothing at all. Alternatively take 271 as the average I.Q. of Yorkshiremen. Go on try it. You'll soon have more sayings than Sheffield has Sithas or London loonies.

Column Wun	*Column Two*	*Column Three*
1. Ell's bells an buckets o'blood	1. Tha munt ever be t'main man at a weddin or a funeral	1. But ahm not ter worry ower much.
2. Sitha	2. There's nowt so queer as folk	2. Tha knows.
3. It's fair cappin but	3. Yer nivver know oo yer friends are	3. Ah reckon.
4. By Ummer but	4. T'int true as work killed no one cost even 'osses turn their arses to it	4. When all said an done.
5. If there's one thing I say	5. Ah'm nobbut fair ter middlin	5. Any on yer can tell.
6. It's past t'time someone said	6. It's thronging wi folk int'snicket	6. Still t'truth nivver urt any-one.
7. By Gum	7. Ale weant work an it weant laike quietly awther	7. Dont yer reckon.
8. Thas got ter admit as ow	8. Possers an set pots'll nivver cum back agean	8. Anyone wi't use of is een can see.
9. Ah must say	9. Chuckin out time int boozers int reet	9. Wouldn't ta say.

These should last you for years!

27

Summat to Speyk

YORKSHER'S the most colourful language in the world because we boil everything down to essentials. Here's a sample of Yorksher wit and wisdom about folk. They may seem a bit rude to you but compliments in Yorkshire are as rare as bacon flavoured crisps at a synagogue. We're trying to help folk improve themselves. So don't say anything nice to a Yorkshire lass or you may have to carry her home. But now us sayings.

We have a lot about meanness because of our dealings with the Scots at York Station and garages on the A1.

Here's some:

> *Ees that mean eed split a current in two.*
> *Ees that tight ee won't let is teeth chatter when ee freezes.*
> *Ees that mean ee wouldn't pee on yer if yer war on fire.*

For restlessness try:

> *As fidgetty as a fly in a bottle.*
> *Buzzing about like a blue arsed fly.*

For laziness:

> *As idle as a Ludlam dog at leans its ead agint wall ter bark.*
> *Ees that idle ee thinks manual labour's a Spanish socialist.*
> *There's more work in a Beecham's pill.*

For clumsiness or awkwardness:

> *Like orse muck, allus int road.*
> *As awkward as Dick's at band at went nine times round an wouldn't tee.*
> *As awkward as a rail out.*
> *As handy as a duck wi a muck fork.*

For someone who talks too much:

> *More rattle than a can o mabs.*
> *Tha talks like an alfpenny book baht leaves.*
> *Tha knows some clog iron.*

A sex maniac can be:

> *As leet geen as a posser head.*
> *As leet geen as a lodging house cat.*

And the really stupid is:

> *Ten pence t't'shilling (**A Nexercise:** Decimalise this).*
> *Ee couldn't it t'barn door sat ont'sneck.*
> *If is brains were dynamite they wouldn't blow is cap off.*

Ee asnt enough sense to come in out oft'rain.
As daft as a brush.
As thick as two short planks.
Ee war gotten in slack watter.

Finally here's a useful collection of phrases to drop in so as to disguise any slight imperfections in your grammar.

Thi mam wants thi booits for loaf tins.   *You have big feet.*

Tha couldn't organise a piss up in a brewery.   *I am not impressed with your competence.*

She's as straight up an down as a yard of pump watter.   *Her bust is not well developed.*

Thas as edgy as a crocodile in an andbag factory.   *You seem nervy.*

She looks as if she tossed a sparrer an lost.   *She shouldn't wear mini skirts.*

Ee's a face like a busted clog.   *He's not Omar Sharif.*

Yer don't look at t'mantlepiece when yer poking t'fire.   *I am far from being so ungallant as to complain about my wife's looks.*

Ee'd eat t'oven door if it were buttered.   *He seems hungry.*

She's got one ye on't pot an another on't chimney.   *She squints.*

Ee's fine as a fart wi a frill on.   *A little overdressed.*

Well there it is. There are lots more but you'll have to go for us course in Advanced Tyke talking.

Vocabulary

ACKERS	Money. As an object of great veneration in Yorkshire money is honoured by having more words to describe it than any other object. See also brass, dosh, gelt, bunce, megs.
ADDLE	Earn as in "addle a living."
ALE	Beer. Up here we toast it this way: "Oft tha's made me friends mi foos Oft tha's made me pop me cloas But noa that thas so near me nose Up that comes an down tha goas."
ATE	To eat. "Summat to ate" is a meat pie, not the time of day.
AXE	To ask, witness the title of the famous question-master on Calendar Commentary, Druit the Mad Axe man.
BACKSLAVVER	Cheek.
BAHN	Going. The Germans copied this for their word "Barnhof" – "do you come here often."

BELT	To hit. Yorkshire is rich in synonyms for this act of necessary correction such as twelt, thrash, fetch 'im 'one, flay, bray, thump, wallop, hammer. Frequent applications are necessary for Southerners, wives and children, particularly other people's, but the Heckmondwike Novelty Co. will shortly be marketing an aerosol twelting can. Huge export sales to Northern Ireland are forecast.
BEVVIED	Boozed up or plea of extenuating circumstances for bashing, gang bashing etc. The richness of the Tyke Tongue is shown by the large number of words for this state of Euphoria such as "three sheets t't'wind," "drunk as a fiddler's fart," "canned up," "cut," "losaked," etc. You ask at the Batley Working Men's Club. They've seen em all, even folk with such a skinful it's running out of their lug holes.
BINT	The low Yorkshireman is deeply religious but his trinity is brass, birds and booze (middle Yorkshiremen are unitarian and believe only in brass). As a major part of this trinity birds are treated with great veneration before marriage, after they're kept in their place (on their backs). So we have a great variety of synonyms such as bird, lass, Judy, etc.
BLETHERING	Conversation of Southerners, Bletherskite, light conversationalist.
BOOZER	Pub. Enter with the gay cry of "Do you serve alcoholic beveridges here". Note that beer costs at least 20p less than in the South.
BRAT	Someone else's child.
BUMBAILIFF	Rent collector. Sad to relate the Mitchell Great, Great, Great Grandfather, Red Bill Sutcliffe was bumbailiff to Colonel Akroyd of Halifax. His uniform now sits in Akroyden Museum. Now few Urban District Councils provide uniforms preferring the men to blend in with the background so as not to attract violence.
CALL	To talk, converse, chat with. Usually used of women since they are allowed to talk among themselves. The word has derogatory overtones as a custom infrequently engaged in.
CLOISE	Field. "Wot noits t'cloise at?" – "What is the condition of the field?"
CODSWALLOP	Party Political Broadcast.
CON. SEC.	Gaffer at t'club. A bloke so important i'Yorkshire that one Sheffield Agent who was trying to get an act of his booked in Las Vegas rang up. "'Ello – is that the Sands 'Otel? Well can I speak t' t'Con. Sec?"
COW CLAP	Cow pat as in the little boy reporting to his mum "Ah seed a cow singing an all't rest war clapping." This at least is better than the fate of Jack Hawkins from Todmorden Social club who was winding his way home sloshed one neet when his cap blew off. He tried on ten cow claps before he found it.
DOFF; DON	Get undressed and dressed. Connected with religious observances in the W.M.C. Sunday lunchtime.

30

DRUFFEN	Drunk. A drunken man is often compared with Canute.
DYKE	Lesbian. Yet it would be dangerous to assume that Black Dyke had anything to do with a lesbian negress.
EE, EEN	Eyes. "I'll wall thi'een up" is not a compliment.
ELBOW GREASE	Effort.
FAFFING	Messing about. Not to be confused with Pfaffing – sewing.
FETTLE	Clean. My grandmother fettled door knocker until it weren't there anymore an used more pumice stone ont'door step than Etna put out in a decade.
FLIBERTYGIBBET	Blatherskite, lightweight, Southerner.
FLUMMOXED	Puzzled.
FRAME	Shape yourself, manage, try.
FRATCH	Fight, argue.
GANSEY	Sweater, pullover, jersey.
GILL	Half pint. In the south a quarter pint.
GINNELL	Narrow passage way. A snicket baht'op. Ginnells begin at Baildon Moor. In Sheffield gennell.
GOB	Mouth.
GORMLESS	Stupid, slow, Southerner.
GUMPTION	Produced only i' Gumption Factories all ower Yorkshire. Not found outside.

In Yorkshire proper few words begin with H.

HOB GOB	Simpleton, Southerner.
HUGGER	Carry.
HUMMER	Curse as in Bloody Hummer – dash it.
KAG HANDED	Left handed, also Keggy handed.
KALIED	Drunk. Another term for which there are many synonyms given its close relationship to that central part of the trinity Booze. Sloshed, Pissed, Cut, Fresh.
KECKS	Pants.
KNACKERED	Whacked, exhausted.
LEET	Light or to like.
LIG	Lie down. In Silsden they're a bit lazy cos the only place to go is Steeton and no one would want to go there. So when the brand new Vicar Rev. Sidebotham went to visit an old lady parishioner he was naturally told by the neighbour "She's gone to liggerdown", "Oh yes, and did the dear lady take the bus or the train" he said.
LOOSING	Ending, breaking up.
LUG	Ear.
MARRIED LIFE	Testicles. As in "I'll ruin yer married life."
MIDDEN	Dunghill or old fashioned earth lavatory. Some people were said to be so lucky if they fell in it they'd come out smelling of roses.
MUCKMENT	Rubbish, Southerner.
NACKERS	Cods, testicles, nuts.
NITHERED	Very cold. A condition found on the kind of day that affects brass monkeys adversely.
NOWT	Opposite of owt. If it warn't for summat there'd be nowt.

31

ON	Engaged in, as in on the game, on the job, on the piss.
PAWSE	Kick. "Must give us pause." (Shakespeare).
PAY	Pea, Pay Cloise – pea field. Daft as a pay cloise – Southerner.
PETTY	Lavatory. In Humanby a new vicar went to visit a local family – to their embarrassment. Mother lectured her four sons on the need to speak proper for the occasion only to have George announce as she served dinner "Gie us a lollock o lean an a lollock o fat while ah gan tit'petty". Despairingly she turned to the vicar "Ahm reet sorry. They an't as much manners as mi arse."
PIGGIN	Lading can.
POSHING	A hiding so a reet poshing isn't going up in the world.
RIG	Back. As ter ever ugged a poak up a stee till thi rig warked?
ROAR	To cry. In Stocksbridge Eli Watmough's wife had just died. Joe his friend went round to sympathise "Ee ahm reet sorry". "Aye" says Eli "ahve been roaring all morning an when ahve ad me dinner ahm going to roar again."
SAM (Verb) or SAMMER	Pick up, collect.
SET POT	Clothes boiler. Copper.
SGONA	Meteorological term as in Sgona rain.
SILING	Pouring with rain. Siling i'stair rods.
SLARTING	Spurting. "Ossin ter slart" – "It's starting to rain."
SLATING	Criticise – slander or pour with rain.
SLUFFENED	Upset.
SNEK	Door fastening.
SNICKET	Narrow passageway, ginnel.
SPICE	Sweets.
STARVED	Frozen. Or hungry as in "Ah'm that starved me belly thinks mi throat's cut." – "Is tea ready?"
SUMMAT	Position of great importance. The nicest thing people can say about you is "Ee is summat." Thus: "If tha'as nowt tha'art nowt, if tha'd 'ad owt tha'd a been summat."
SUP	Drink.
TEEM	Crowded, teeming wi folk.
THRONG	Crowd: e.g. "thronging wi folk" or very busy e.g. "Throng as Throp's wife when she hanged hersen wit'dishclout."
UPT SPOUT	Pregnant.
WARK	Ache as in Back wark, Belly wark or Bellywak.
WARPHEAD	Dimwit, Southerner. Warphead is the beam on the warp weaving loom.
WHILE	Until. Tragedy struck on a new crossing in the North Riding which carried the sign "Do not cross while red light is on". Huge queues formed at the cross signal and poured over while the light was red.
WITTER	Natter 'in Lancashire-Maether' as in Maether Macree.
YAR	In Bradford "your" but in Huddersfield "our" a situation which has led to a lot of confusion at Rugby League matches when advice is proferred on who should have a girder hacked off.

32